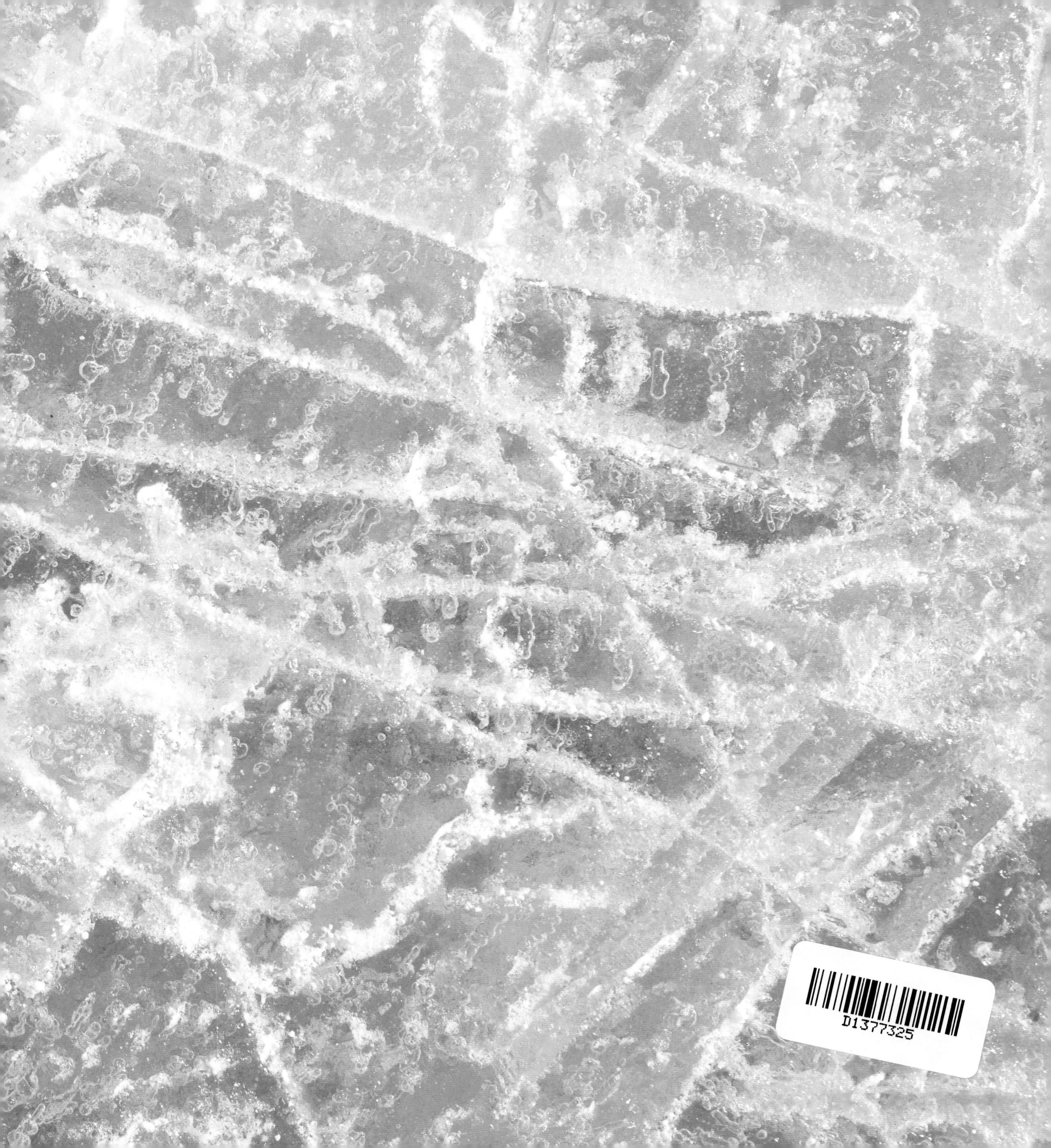

THE WONDER OF PENGUINS & POLAR CREATURES

THE WONDER OF PENGUINS & POLAR CREATURES

Published by Fog City Press,
a division of Weldon Owen Inc.
1045 Sansome Street, Suite 100
San Francisco, CA 94111 USA

www.weldonowen.com

weldon**owen**

President & Publisher Roger Shaw
SVP, Sales & Marketing Amy Kaneko
Finance & Operations Director Philip Paulick
Senior Editor Lucie Parker
Editorial Assistant Molly O'Neil Stewart
Creative Director Kelly Booth
Designer Meghan Hildebrand
Senior Production Designer Rachel Lopez Metzger
Production Director Chris Hemesath
Associate Production Director Michelle Duggan
Imaging Manager Don Hill

Weldon Owen is a division of Bonnier USA

Library of Congress Cataloging in Publication data is available.

ISBN 13: 978-1-68188-255-0

10 9 8 7 6 5 4 3 2 1
2017 2018 2019 2020 2021

Printed in China

INTRODUCTION

The Arctic is a cold, cold place—but it's full of fascinating animals ready to brave the snow and ice!

There are penguins, wolves, whales, and more. Many have special fur, feathers, and claws that help them adapt to the weather and hunt for food in the icy winters.

Let's get to know these winter warriors of the polar regions!

Most penguins live in cold places. They are kept warm by their feathers and a thick layer of fat under their skins.

Fun Fact
There are at least 17 different types of penguins.

Fun Fact

Sometimes penguins gather in large groups called colonies.

Penguins like to huddle together for warmth. They take turns being at the center.

Fun Fact

Baby penguins' feathers change color as they age.

Penguin chicks' soft feathers are not waterproof, but they keep the chicks warm.

An Arctic fox's
fur changes color
with the seasons—
white for winter
and brown-gray
for summer.

Fun Fact

In the winter, brown stoats become white and are called ermines.

Fun Fact

Female snowy owls' feathers have more brown dots than males'.

Like many of the
other animals
that live in
snowy places,
lots of polar birds
are white.

The world's smallest penguins have blue feathers and are around 16 inches (40 cm) tall.

Fun Fact

In Australia, they call these penguins fairy penguins.

Puffins' beaks aren't just colorful. They can hold a few small fish at once—very handy for bringing food to their babies.

Fun Fact

Puffins shed the colorful parts of their beaks.

Fun Fact

Rockhoppers hop because they can't do belly slides.

These rockhoppers (left) and macaronis (above) have crests of colorful feathers on their heads.

Musk oxen,
caribou, and Dall
rams have horns
and antlers on
their heads to
protect themselves
from danger.

Fun Fact

Caribou is another word for reindeer.

Penguins waddle when they walk because they use their tails and flippers to help them balance.

Fun Fact

Penguins' wings are called flippers, which they use to swim.

Fun Fact

Some penguins walk in straight lines to the sea.

Penguins have claws on their webbed feet to help them walk on ice and snow.

Fun Fact

Black backs and white bellies help with camouflage.

African penguins' spots are unique, much like human fingerprints.

Fun Fact

Polar bear pups always stay close to their mothers.

Polar bears do most of their hunting underwater. When they're on land, they tend to sleep and take it easy.

Polar bears and seals don't have blowholes. But they're pretty good at holding their breath while hunting underwater.

Fun Fact

Seals have front and back flippers for land and sea.

All kinds of whales
live in and visit
the Arctic's cold,
cold water, like
belugas, orcas,
and humpbacks.

Fun Fact

When humpback whales breach, they make a big splash. The bubbles make a "net" that traps food.

Fun Fact

Female walruses are called cows, males are known as bulls, and the babies are called calfs.

Adult walruses have two big teeth called tusks. They help them climb out from the water onto ice.

When seals grow up, their fur becomes a darker color. This means they stand out more in the snow, but they blend in when they're swimming!

Fun Fact

Seals love to lie out and keep warm by sunbathing.

Fun Fact

Like many birds, adult penguins feed chewed-up food to their chicks.

Penguin parents also take turns holding their chicks and eggs on their feet to warm them.

Fun Fact
Penguins use beaks
and flippers to
groom each other.

The male penguin's mating call sounds like trumpet blasts. Couples often stay together for life.

Watch out!
Wolverines, wolves,
and wild dogs are
out there too!

Fun Fact

Wolves howl to find their family, which is called a pack.

All photos courtesy of Shutterstock with the exception of:
Andrea London Ltd.: 43 ArcticPhoto/Ecocepts International: 11t
ArcticPhoto/B&C Alexander: 31t Dreamstime: 5, 14t, 17t, 39b
iStock: 11b , 14b, 16, 22, 23t, 24t, 24b, 29, 30, 32, 33t, 40b,
42, 44, 46t Lucky Oliver: 33b